Table of Contents

About the Visualforce Workbook

Visualforce is a framework that allows developers to build sophisticated, custom user interfaces that can be hosted natively on the Force.com platform. This workbook provides a gentle introduction to many of the features in Visualforce.

You will learn how to build user interfaces that look like the standard user interfaces provided by Force.com, as well as how to build your own user interfaces with full pixel-level control. Along the way you'll find out how to create components, reusable pieces of Visualforce, as well as how to hook Visualforce into your applications. You'll also learn about the Model–View–Controller (MVC) foundations of Visualforce, and use a little Apex code.

The goal of this workbook is to give you a tour of many of the features of Visualforce, not to build a working application. While touring along, feel free to experiment; change the code a little, substitute different components—and have fun!

Intended Audience

This workbook is intended for web developers new to the Force.com platform who want an introduction to web development on the platform, and for Salesforce admins who want to delve more deeply into app development using coding. If you're an admin just getting started with Force.com, see the Force.com Platform Fundamentals for an introduction to point-and-click app development.

Workbook Version

This workbook is updated for Summer '12, and was last revised on June 14, 2012. You should be able to successfully complete all of the tutorials using the Summer '12 version of Force.com (API version 25.0).

To download the latest version of this workbook, go to http://developer.force.com/workbooks.

Supported Browsers

Browser	Comments
Microsoft® Internet Explorer® versions 7, 8, and 9	If you use Internet Explorer, Salesforce recommends using the latest version. Apply all Microsoft hotfixes. The compatibility view feature in Internet Explorer 8 and 9 is not supported in Salesforce. For configuration recommendations, see "Configuring Internet Explorer" in the online help.
Mozilla® Firefox®, most recent stable version	Salesforce.com makes every effort to test and support the most recent version of Firefox. For configuration recommendations, see "Configuring Firefox" in the online help.
Google Chrome™, most recent stable version	Google Chrome applies updates automatically; Salesforce.com makes every effort to test and support the most recent version. There are no configuration recommendations for Chrome. Chrome is not supported for the Console tab or the **Add Google Doc to Salesforce** browser button.
Google Chrome Frame™ plug-in for Microsoft® Internet Explorer® 6	Supported plug-in for Internet Explorer 6 only. Google Chrome Frame applies updates automatically; Salesforce.com supports only the most recent version. For configuration recommendations, see "Installing Google Chrome Frame for Microsoft® Internet Explorer®" in the online help. Chrome Frame plug-in is not supported for the Service Cloud console or Forecasts.
Apple® Safari® version 5.1.x	There are no configuration recommendations for Safari. Safari is not supported for the Salesforce CRM Call Center CTI Toolkit or the Service Cloud console.

Before You Begin

These tutorials are designed to work with a Force.com Developer Edition organization, or *DE org* for short. DE orgs are multipurpose environments with all of the features and permissions that allow you to develop, package, test, and install apps. You can get your own DE org for free at http://developer.force.com/join, and you can use the techniques that you learn in this workbook in all Force.com environments that support development.

It would also help to have a little context by learning a little about Force.com itself, which you can find in the first few tutorials of the Force.com Workbook.

After You Finish

After you finish the workbook, you'll be ready to explore a lot more Visualforce and Force.com development:

- Learn more about Force.com and Visualforce from the companion Force.com Workbook at http://developer.force.com/workbooks.
- Download the Visualforce Cheat Sheet at http://developer.force.com/cheatsheets.
- Get in-depth documentation for Visualforce in the *Visualforce Developer's Guide*.
- Start learning the Apex programming language with the Apex Workbook.
- Discover more Force.com and access articles, documentation, and code samples by visiting Developer Force at http://developer.force.com.

Tutorial #1: Creating and Listing Visualforce Pages

In this tutorial, you will learn how to create and edit your first Visualforce page. The page will be really simple, but this is the start, and we'll soon expand on it. Along the way you'll familiarize yourself with the editor and automatic page creation.

Before you start, please create a free Force.com Developer Edition Environment, as indicated earlier in the "Before you Begin" section.

Step 1: Enable Visualforce Development Mode

Development mode embeds a Visualforce page editor in your browser that allows you to see code and preview the page at the same time. Development mode also adds an Apex editor for editing controllers and extensions.

1. Click **Your Name** > **Setup** > **My Personal Information** > **Personal Information**.
2. Click **Edit**.
3. Select the Development Mode checkbox, then click **Save**.

Step 2: Create a Visualforce Page

Now you are ready to create your first Visualforce page:

1. In your browser, add `/apex/hello` to the URL for your Salesforce instance. For example, if your Salesforce instance is `https://na1.salesforce.com`, the new URL is `https://na1.salesforce.com/apex/hello`. You will see the following error:

Visualforce Error

Page hello does not exist

 Create Page hello

2. Click the **Create Page hello** link to create the new page. You will see your new page with some default markup.

 Note: If you don't see the Page Editor below the page, just click the **hello** tab in the status bar.

That's it! The page includes some default text, as well as an embedded page editor displaying the source code. This is the primary way you'll be creating pages throughout this workbook.

Step 3: Edit the Visualforce Page

Now that you've created the Visualforce page, you need to customize it for your own use. You can edit and preview the changes in real time.

1. You don't want the heading of the page to say "Congratulations," so change the contents of the `<h1>` tag to Hello World, remove the comments, and the "This is your new page" text. The code now looks like this:

    ```
    <apex:page>
        <h1>Hello World</h1>
    </apex:page>
    ```

2. Click the **Save** button at the top of the Page Editor.

The page reloads to reflect your changes. Note that Hello World appears in a large font. This is because of the `<h1>` tag—a standard HTML tag. Visualforce pages are generally composed of two types of tags: tags that identify Visualforce components (such as `<apex:page>`), and tags that are standard HTML.

Development mode, which you enabled in Step 1, makes development fast and easy. You can simply make changes, press Save, and immediately see the changes reflected. You can use a keyboard shortcut too—click CTRL+S to save at any time. You can also click the editor minimize button to see the full page.

When you deploy the page in a production environment, or if you switch off development mode, the editor will no longer be available.

Step 4: Find all Visualforce Pages

Now that you've created a Visualforce page, you'll need to know where to find it.

1. Click **Your Name** > **Setup** > **Develop** > **Pages**.
2. Scroll down to locate the page created in Step 2—`hello`.

This views your page, and even allows you to edit it. However, this editor is different from the one we've seen in the previous steps—it also doesn't let you immediately view the changes (unless you have the page open in a separate tab).

Step 5: Alternative Page Creation

You can also create a new page from this listing, and then edit it just like you did in Step 2 by navigating to the correct URL—taking into account the name of the page you created. Try it!

1. Go to **Your Name** > **Setup** > **Develop** > **Pages**, then click **New**.
2. Create and label the page `hello2`.
3. Click **Save**.
4. Navigate to the new page using the URL as you did in Step 2: `https://your-salesforce-instance/apex/hello2`

The Visualforce editor in Setup is good to know about, and a great way to see all your pages. However, the development mode editor we used in previous steps is more powerful, and lets you view your changes immediately. We'll use it for the rest of this workbook.

Summary

You now know how to enable development mode, and list and create Visualforce pages. In the next tutorial, you'll learn a little about the page editor, and the basics of Visualforce components, which are the building blocks of any page.

Tutorial #2: Adding Attributes and Using Auto-Suggest

The page you created in Tutorial #1 shares a characteristic of every Visualforce page—it starts and ends with the `<apex:page>` tag. `<apex:page>` is actually a Visualforce component—and one that must always be present. So all Visualforce pages will look similar to this:

```
<apex:page>
    Your Stuff Here
</apex:page>
```

Note the use of angle brackets, as well as how you indicate where a component starts and ends. The start is simply the component name in angle brackets: `<apex:page>`. The end is the component name prepended with a '/' character in angle brackets: `</apex:page>`. All Visualforce pages follow this same convention—requiring that the pages you create be "well-formed XML" (with a few exceptions). A few components are self-closing—they have this form: `<apex:detail />` (note the position of the /). Think of that as a start and end tag wrapped up in one!

You can generally modify the behavior and/or appearance of a component by adding attributes. These are name/value pairs that sit within the start tag. For example, here's an attribute: `sidebar="false"`.

Step 1: Add Attributes Using Auto-Suggest

Let's play some more with our first hello page. It turns out that the sidebar attribute is a valid attribute for the `<apex:page>` component.

1. Add `sidebar="false"` within the start tag of the `<apex:page>` component as follows:

    ```
    <apex:page sidebar="false">
    ```

2. Click **Save**.

    Notice that the left hand area of your page has changed—the sidebar has been removed. In effect, the sidebar attribute modifies the behavior and appearance of the `<apex:page>` component.

8

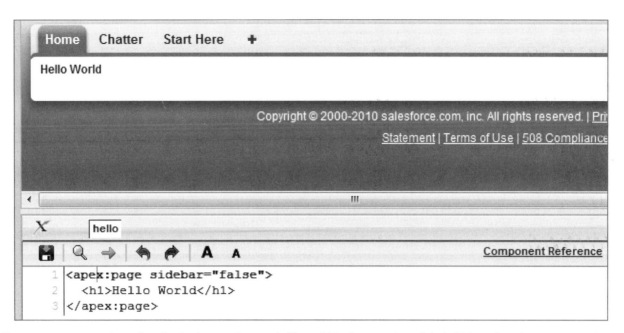

3. Position your cursor just after the final quotation mark ("), and hit the space bar. A helpful list of attributes pop up that are valid for the `<apex:page>` component. Choose the `showHeader` attribute.

4. The attribute is automatically added to your page, and you now need to supply a value for the attribute. Add `false`. Your complete first line should look like this:

```
<apex:page sidebar="false" showHeader="false">
```

5. Click **Save** (remember, you can also press CTRL+S as a shortcut).

   This time your page looks completely different. By setting the `showHeader` attribute to false, you've not only removed the top header, but all the default styling associated with the page.

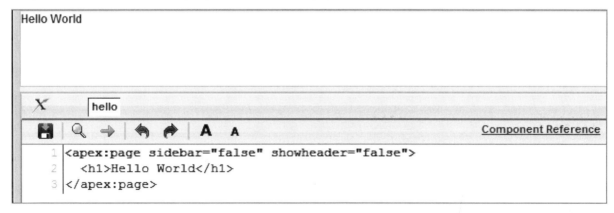

Let's put it back the way it was—having the top header is very useful during development.

6. Change the `showHeader` attribute's value to `true`.

7. Click **Save**.

Step 2: Add Additional Components

You've created a page, used the `<apex:page>` component, and changed its behavior. You'll typically want to use additional components that supply a lot more functionality.

Visualforce comes with a few dozen built-in components, and you can install and build your own components to extend this set. In this lesson you'll learn how to locate them, and use one.

1. Click the **Component Reference** link in the Page Editor. A help popup window displays with all available components.
2. Click `<apex:pageBlock>`. A description of what the component does, and what attributes you can add to change its behavior displays in the Component Details tab.
3. Click the Usage tab to see an example of how to use the component. You'll notice that the `<apex:pageBlock>` component is often used with the `<apex:pageBlockSection>` component. Click `<apex:pageBlockSection>` to learn more about that component.

   In general, you'll dip into the component reference whenever you need to. You'll soon learn what the major components do—and while some of them take a large number of attributes, in practice you will only use a handful.

   Now add both components to your page. We're going to go a little faster here—see if you can do this without looking at the final code below:

4. Within the `<apex:page>` component, add an `<apex:pageBlock>` component with a `title` attribute set to `A Block Title`.
5. Within the `<apex:pageBlock>` component, add an `<apex:pageBlockSection>` component, with its `title` attribute set to `A Section Title`.
6. Within the `<apex:pageBlockSection>`, add some text, like `I'm three components deep!`
7. Click **Save**. Your final code will look something like this:

```
<apex:page sidebar="false">
    <apex:pageBlock title="A Block Title">
        <apex:pageBlockSection title="A Section Title">
            I'm three components deep!
        </apex:pageBlockSection>
    </apex:pageBlock>
</apex:page>
```

The final page will look something like this:

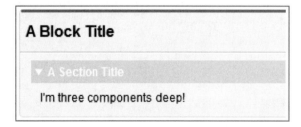

You can click the tiny disclosure triangle next to A Section Title to minimize that section of the block.

Step 3: Add Nested Components

Adding additional components is easy.

1. Navigate to the end of the `<apex:pageBlockSection>` component, and add another `<apex:pageBlockSection>` component with its own title. Both `<apex:pageBlockSection>` components must be contained within the same `<apex:pageBlock>` component.
2. Click **Save** and admire your handiwork.

```
<apex:page sidebar="false">
    <apex:pageBlock title="A Block Title">
        <apex:pageBlockSection title="A Section Title">
            I'm three components deep!
        </apex:pageBlockSection>
        <apex:pageBlockSection title="A New Section">
            This is another section.
        </apex:pageBlockSection>
    </apex:pageBlock>
</apex:page>
```

Note the number of "nested" components. The start and the end tag for an `<apex:pageBlockSection>` are both within the start and end tag for the `<apex:pageBlock>` component. And your first `<apex:pageBlockSection>` ends before the next one starts (its end tag, `</apex:pageBlockSection>`, appears before the start of the new one, `<apex:pageBlockSection>`). All of the components on a Visualforce page tend to nest in this way—and the editor tells you when you've made a mistake (for example, if you forget an end tag).

Summary

In this tutorial you learned how to change the behavior and appearance of Visualforce components by adding attributes, how to use the auto-suggest feature of the editor, and how to use the Component Reference to look up additional components. You also learned that Visualforce components are often nested within each other.

Learning More

Here are additional Visualforce components that let you build pages that match the platform visual style:

- `<apex:pageBlockButtons>` lets you provide a set of buttons that are styled like standard user interface buttons
- The optional `<apex:pageBlockSectionItem>` represents a single piece of data in a `<apex:pageBlockSection>`
- `<apex:tabPanel>`, `<apex:toolbar>`, and `<apex:panelGrid>` provide other ways of grouping information on a page

Tutorial #3: Understanding Simple Variables and Formulas

The Visualforce pages you've created so far have been static. In general, Visualforce pages are dynamic—they can display data retrieved from the database, or data that changes depending on who is logged on and viewing the page. They can become dynamic through the use of variables and formulas.

This tutorial introduces you to variables, formulas and the expression language syntax used in Visualforce. Variables typically contain information that you have retrieved from objects in the Force.com database, or which the platform has made available to you—for example, the name of the logged-in user. A number of built-in formulas are available to add functionality to your page—you'll discover some basic formulas in this tutorial too.

Step 1: Global Variables

Force.com retains information about the logged-in user in a variable called User. You can access fields of this User variable (and any others) by using a special expression language syntax: `{! $<global variable>.<field name>}`

1. Modify your existing page to include the following line: `{! $User.FirstName}`. Remember that any content must lie within the `<apex:page>` component (between its open and closing tags).
2. Click **Save**.

Your Visualforce page looks something like this:

```
<apex:page sidebar="false">
    {! $User.FirstName}
</apex:page>
```

In the future we'll assume that you know to put any Visualforce markup within the `<apex:page>` tag. We'll also assume that by now you're comfortable enough to "Click Save" and view the result as well!

The `{! ... }` tells Visualforce that whatever lies within the braces is dynamic and written in the expression language, and its value must be calculated and substituted at run time when someone views the page. Visualforce is case-insensitive, and spaces within the `{! ... }` syntax are also ignored. So this is just as effective: `{!$USER.firstname}`.

Here's how to show the first name and last name of the logged-in user: `{! $User.FirstName} {! $User.LastName}`

Step 2: Basic Formulas

Visualforce lets you embed more than just variables in the expression language. It also supports formulas that let you manipulate values. The `&` character is the formula language operator that concatenates strings.

1. Add this to your Visualforce page: `{! $User.firstname & ' ' & $User.lastname}`

   This tells Visualforce to retrieve the firstname and lastname fields from the global User object, and to concatenate them with a space character. The output will be something like: Joe Bloggs.

   In general, formulas are slightly more advanced and have a simple syntax that includes the function name, a set of parentheses, and an optional set of parameters.

2. Add this to your Visualforce page:

```
<p> Today's Date is {! TODAY()} </p>
<p> Next week it will be {! TODAY() + 7} </p>
```

You'll see something like this in the output:

```
Today's Date is Wed Feb 08 00:00:00 GMT 2012
Next week it will be Wed Feb 15 00:00:00 GMT 2012
```

The <p> tags are standard HTML for creating paragraphs. In other words, we wanted both sentences to be in individual paragraphs, not all on one line. The TODAY() function returns the current date as a date data type. Note how the time values are all set to 0. Also note the + operator on the date. The expression language assumes you want to add days, so it added 7 days to the date.

3. You can use functions as parameters in other functions, and also have functions that take multiple parameters too. Add this:

```
<p>The year today is {! YEAR(TODAY())}</p>
<p>Tomorrow will be day number  {! DAY(TODAY() + 1)}</p>
<p>Let's find a maximum: {! MAX(1,2,3,4,5,6,5,4,3,2,1)} </p>
<p>The square root of 49 is {! SQRT(49)}</p>
<p>Is it true?  {! CONTAINS('salesforce.com', 'force.com')}</p>
```

The output will look something like this:

```
The year today is 2012
Tomorrow will be day number 9
Let's find a maximum: 6
The square root of 49 is 7.0
Is it true? true
```

The CONTAINS() function returns a boolean value: something that is either true or false. It compares two arguments of text and returns true if the first argument contains the second argument. If not, it returns false. In this case, the string "force.com" is contained within the string "salesforce.com", so it returns true.

Step 3: Conditionals

Sometimes you want to display something dynamically, based on the value of an expression. For example, if an invoice has no line items, you might want to display the word "none" instead of an empty list, or if some item has expired, you might want to display "late" instead of showing the due date.

You can do this in Visualforce by using a conditional formula expression, such as IF(). The IF() expression takes three arguments:

- The first is a boolean: something that is either true or false. You've seen an example of that in the CONTAINS() function.
- The second argument is something that will be returned if the boolean is true.
- The third argument is something that will be returned if the boolean is false.

Insert the following and try to predict what will be displayed if you save the page:

```
{! IF ( CONTAINS('salesforce.com','force.com'), 'Yep', 'Nah') }
{! IF ( DAY(TODAY()) > 14, 'After the 14th', 'On or before the 14th') }
```

You'll see something like this:

```
Yep
On or before the 14th
```

Of course, this all depends on when you run the code. After the 14th in a month, it looks different.

Summary

Visualforce lets you embed operations that evaluate at runtime using a special expression language syntax: `{! expression}`. Global variables are accessed using the `$VariableName` syntax. The expression language lets you manipulate strings, numbers, text, and dates, as well as conditionally execute operations.

Learning More

- The Formulas Cheat Sheet provides a concise guide to the many formulas you can use.
- The Visualforce Developer's Guide has a lot more detail on formulas.

Tutorial #4: Using Standard Controllers

Visualforce's Model-View-Controller (MVC) design pattern makes it easy to separate the view and its styling from the underlying database and logic. In MVC, the view (the Visualforce page) interacts with a controller. In our case, the controller is usually an Apex class, which exposes some functionality to the page. For example, the controller can contain the logic to be executed when a button is clicked. A controller also typically interacts with the model (the database)—making available data that the view might want to display.

Most Force.com objects have default standard controllers that can be used to interact with the data associated with the object, so in many cases you don't need to write the code for the controller yourself. You can extend the standard controllers to add new functionality, or create custom controllers from scratch. In this tutorial, you'll learn about the standard controllers.

Step 1: Find Identifiers of Records

When your Visualforce pages interact with other pages in your application, you can automatically pass in the record's identifier, and your Visualforce page can then display that data. Right now your pages are stand-alone, so for your page to display data from a record in the database, it needs to know the record's identifier.

Your Developer Edition environment has a number of objects that store data, available out of the box.

1. For example, switch to the Sales application by choosing **Sales** from the drop down.
2. Now select the Accounts tab. Ensure the pick list shows All Accounts and click **Go** to view all the account records.

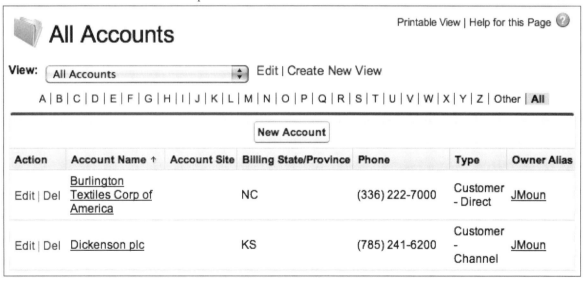

3. Click Burlington Textiles (or any other record) to view the details. Your screen displays all the details for that account:

Notice that your URL has changed—it now looks something like this: `https://<your salesforce instance>.salesforce.com/0018000000MDfn1`

The identifier is that series of digits at the end, in this case, 0018000000MDfn1. The identifier, or ID as it's often written, is unique across all records in your database. If you know the ID for any record, and have permission, you can often construct a URL to view it by replacing 0018000000MDfn1 with the record's identifier.

When you visited `https://<salesforce instance>.salesforce.com/0018000000MDfn1`, Force.com automatically retrieved the record with identifier 0018000000MDfn1 from the database, and automatically constructed a user interface for it. In the other lessons in this tutorial, you're going to take away some of the automation, and create your own user interface.

Step 2: Display Data from a Record

Create a new Visualforce page, `accountDisplay`, with the following content:

```
<apex:page standardController="Account">
    <p>Hello {! $User.FirstName}!</p>
    <p>You are viewing the {! account.name} account.</p>
</apex:page>
```

You'll recognize the `{! }` expression syntax from the previous tutorial, and that `$User.FirstName` refers to the First Name field of the User global variable. There are a few new things though:

1. The `standardController="Account"` attribute tells Visualforce to use an automatically-generated controller for the Account object, and to provide access to the controller in the Visualforce page.
2. The `{! account.name}` expression retrieves the value of the account variable's name field. The account variable is automatically made available by the standard controller (it's named after the standard controller's name).

Controllers generally have logic that handles button clicks and interacts with the database. By using the `standardController` attribute, your Visualforce page has access to a rich controller that is automatically generated for you.

The standard controller for the Account object determines when an identifier is being used in the page, and if it is, queries the database and retrieves the record associated with that identifier. It then assigns that record to the account variable so that you can do as you please with the data in your Visualforce page.

When you click **Save**, you will see your first name and an empty account name. This is because you haven't told the Visualforce page which account record to display. Go to your URL and modify it so that you include the ID from Step 1. So instead of something like:

```
https://na3.salesforce.com/apex/accountDisplay
```

change it to something like:

```
https://na3.salesforce.com/apex/accountDisplay?id=0018000000MDfn1
```

In your case, change the identifier 0018000000MDfn1 to whatever you found in Step 1. You might need to change "na3" as well, to whatever your salesforce instance currently is.

Now when you save your work, the account name displays:

> Hello Jon!
>
> You are viewing the Burlington Textiles Corp of America account.

Step 3: Display Other Fields

Your `accountDisplay` page only displays the name field of the Account object. To find other fields to display for the object, go to **Setup > Customize > Accounts > Fields**. Click any field, such as Ticker Symbol. The Field Name field provides the name that you can use in your own Visualforce pages. For example, for this particular field, the name is TickerSymbol.

Modify accountDisplay to include this field by adding the following paragraph after the existing one:

```
<p>Here's the Ticker Symbol field: {! account.TickerSymbol}</p>
```

Step 4: Display Fields from Related Records

You can also display data from related records. For example, while viewing the object details for Account, you might have noticed that the Account object has a field called Account Owner, and that its type is Lookup(User). In other words, this field has a relationship to a User record. By clicking the Account Owner field label link, you'll discover its Field Name is *Owner*.

The Owner relationship represents a User. And, if you click **Customize** > **Users** > **Fields**, you'll find that User has a Name field. Let's use this information to display it.

1. Modify `accountDisplay` to include this field by adding the following paragraph after the existing one:

```
<p>Here's the owner of this account: {! account.Owner.Name}</p>
```

The "dot notation" (`account.Owner.Name`) indicates that you want to traverse the relationship between the records. You know that `account.Owner` indicates the Owner field of the account record. The extra name at the end indicates that the owner field isn't a simple field representing a String, but a relationship to another record (it's a Lookup(User)), and that you'd like to get the record represented by the value of the Owner field (it's a User record), and display the Name field on that record.

 Tip: If you've created your own custom objects (instead of using objects like Account) and want to know how to reference a field, you have to follow a slightly different procedure. Click **Setup** > **Create** > **Objects**, select your object, and then the field. The API Name now indicates the name of the field that you must use in your Visualforce pages. For example, if your field was called *Foo*, its API Name is *Foo__c*, and you'd reference it with that name—something like: `{! myobject__c.foo__c}`.

Summary

Standard controllers provide basic, out-of-the-box, controller functionality, including automatic record retrieval. This tutorial showed how to locate the identifier for a record and use the standard controller to display the record's data. The standard controller also contains functionality to save or update a record, which you'll see later.

Learning More

Visualforce also supports standard list controllers, which allow you to create Visualforce pages that can display or act on a set of records, with pagination.

Tutorial #5: Using Standard User Interface Components

In Tutorial #2: Adding Attributes and Using Auto-Suggest you learned about the `<apex:pageBlockSection>` component, and in the previous tutorial you learned how to show some data from an Account record using the expression language. In this tutorial you'll discover additional Visualforce components that produce output that looks and feels like the automatically-generated user interfaces.

Step 1: Display a Record or Related Lists

Creating a list of records is as easy as typing up a single component.

1. Modify your `accountDisplay` Visualforce page to look like this:

    ```
    <apex:page standardController="Account">
        <apex:detail/>
    </apex:page>
    ```

    If you access your page with a valid account ID passed in as a parameter, as demonstrated in the previous tutorial (it will look something like this: `https://na3.salesforce.com/apex/AccountDisplay?id=0018000000MDfn1`), then you'll see a lot of output.

2. The `<apex:detail/>` component displays the standard view page for a record. It shows related lists as well, such as contacts. You can switch these off by adding the `relatedList="false"` attribute. Try adding it, click **Save**, and spot the difference.

3. You can show only a particular related list; such as the list of case records that are related to the account record you are viewing. Add the following tag:

    ```
    <apex:relatedList list="Cases" />
    ```

Cases			New Case
Action	**Case**	**Contact Name**	**Subject**
Edit | Cls	00001019	Jack Rogers	Structural failure of generator base
Edit | Cls	00001020	Jack Rogers	Power generation below stated level

Although these tags are very simple, they're doing a lot of work for you—and relying on that standard controller to go and retrieve the data. Sometimes, however, you want more control over page layout.

Step 2: Display Fields

If you want to selectively determine a record's fields for display, use the `<apex:outputField>` component. This component, when embedded in the `<apex:pageBlock>` component, displays not only the value of the field, but also the field's label.

1. Insert the following into your page to see it in action:

```
<apex:pageBlock title="Custom Output">
    <apex:pageBlockSection title="Custom Section Title">
        <apex:outputField value="{!account.Name}"/>
        <apex:outputField value="{!account.Owner.Name}"/>
    </apex:pageBlockSection>
</apex:pageBlock>
```

Here, `account.Name` specifies the current account record's name field, whereas `account.Owner.Name` looks at the owner field of the account record, and then retrieves that record's name field.

Step 3: Display a Table

In the previous lessons, you displayed individual fields and a complete record. Sometimes however, you need to display a set of fields across a number of records—for example, the list of contacts associated with the account. In this step you will list the contacts of an account record by iterating over the list and displaying each one individually. It may seem complex initially because there are multiple tags that nest within each other, but you will find it second nature in no time. Don't forget you can always click the **Component Reference** link to learn more about each.

1. First start by adding an `<apex:pageBlock>` component:

```
<apex:pageBlock title="My Account Contacts">
</apex:pageBlock>
```

2. You can save and view the result if you like. Now within this component, insert another one, the `<apex:pageBlockTable>` component:

```
<apex:pageBlockTable value="{! account.contacts}" var="item">
</apex:pageBlockTable>
```

You can think of this component as doing the following: it takes a look at its `value` attribute, and retrieves the list of records that it finds there. In this case, it retrieves the `contacts` field that represents the list of Contact records associated with the current Account record. Then, for each individual Contact record, it assigns it to a variable called `item`. It does this repeatedly until it reaches the end of the list. The key lies in the body of the component. This will be output at each iteration—effectively allowing you to produce something for each individual record.

3. Ideally, you want to insert something inside of the `<apex:pageBlockTable>` component that does something with the current item. Try adding this:

```
<apex:column value="{! item.name}"/>
```

The `<apex:column>` component creates a new column within the table. It adds a table header based on the name of the field, and also outputs the values for that field in the rows of the table, one row per record. In this case, you have specified `{! item.name}`, which will show the name field for each of the Account's Contacts.

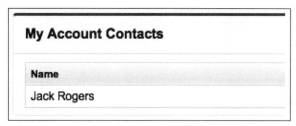

Here's what your final code looks like:

```
<apex:pageBlock title="My Account Contacts">
    <apex:pageBlockTable value="{! account.contacts}" var="item">
        <apex:column value="{! item.name}"/>
    </apex:pageBlockTable>
</apex:pageBlock>
```

Contact records also have a field called phone. Try adding a column to display the phone numbers. Of course, if you don't have any contacts associated with the account that you're viewing, or if you haven't supplied an account ID, then it won't display anything.

Summary

The `<apex:detail>` and `<apex:relatedList>` components make it tremendously easy to display records and related lists by utilizing the standard controller to automatically retrieve the record's data. The `<apex:pageBlockTable>` component provides a way to iterate over a list of records, producing output for each record in the list.

Learning More

- Use `<apex:facet>` to customize the caption, headers and footers of a table.
- The `<apex:enhancedList>` and `<apex:listViews>` components provide a way to embed a standard list view of an object's records.

Tutorial #6: Overriding and Pointing to Pages

Using Visualforce, you can override pretty much any aspect of the user interface, such as buttons, tabs, or links.

In this tutorial, you'll explore how to use Visualforce pages that you've created to replace standard Salesforce behavior.

Step 1: Override the Standard Display for a Page

The Visualforce page you created in Tutorial #4: Using Standard Controllers can function as a replacement to the standard detail page for an account. You can modify the standard user interface generated by the platform to ensure that your page gets shown instead of the standard page.

1. Click **Setup** > **Customize** > **Accounts** > **Buttons and Links**.
2. Click **Edit** next to the View item in the Standard Buttons and Links list.
3. For **Override With**, select Visualforce Page.
4. From the Visualforce Page drop-down list, select accountDisplay.
5. Click **Save**.

To see this in action, select the Accounts tab and then choose an account. Your page displays instead of the default. You've successfully configured the platform to automatically pass in that ID parameter to your page.

6. Follow the same procedure to reverse the override, so you can view the default page on the next lesson.

Step 2: Embed a Page on a Standard Layout

Another way to get your page displayed is to embed it within a standard layout for another page. For example, imagine your `accountDisplay` showed an interesting analysis of the account data, and you wanted to embed it within the standard account detail view.

1. Click **Setup** > **Customize** > **Accounts** > **Page Layouts**.
2. Click **Edit** next to Account Layout.
3. Select Visualforce Pages in the left column of the user interface elements palette.
4. You'll notice your page appears here (because it uses the Accounts standard controller).
5. Select `accountDisplay`, and drag it to the Account Information panel.
6. Click **Save**.
7. To see this in action, select the Accounts tab and then choose an account. You'll notice the standard display of data, with your Visualforce page embedded within it! Your embedded page ideally needs to accommodate the inline display, so it might look a little plain right now, but notice how the embedded page automatically shows data of the same record—it's also being passed the ID parameter.

Step 3: Create a Button that Links to a Visualforce Page

Pages like the standard account detail page have buttons, such as Edit and Delete. You can add a new button here that links to *your* page.

1. Click **Setup** > **Customize** > **Accounts** > **Buttons and Links**.
2. In Custom Buttons and Links, click **New**.
3. Enter `MyButton` for the **Label**.
4. Enter `My_Button` for the **Name**.
5. For the Display Type, select **Detail Page Button**.
6. Select Visualforce Page in the **Content Source** picklist.
7. In the Content picklist that appears, select your `accountDisplay` page.
8. Click **Save**.

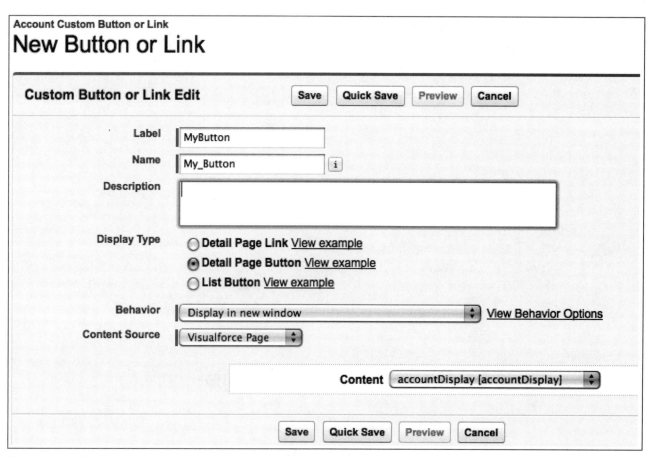

9. Now that you have your button, you need to add it to a page layout. Repeat the process from Step 2: Embed a Page on a Standard Layout but, instead of selecting a Visualforce Page, add a Button, and select **MyButton**.

 Note: Depending on your browser settings, you might get a privacy warning—simply allow your browser to load pages from the Visualforce domain to avoid these warnings.

You can use a similar procedure to create a link, instead of a button, and you can add many buttons and links to standard and custom pages to create just the right navigation and user interface for your app.

Step 4: Create Hyperlinks to URLs or Other Visualforce Pages

You might want to point from one Visualforce page to another, or to an external URL.

1. Modify your Visualforce page to include the `<apex:outputlink>` component to produce a link:

```
<apex:outputLink value="http://developer.force.com/">Click me!</apex:outputLink>
```

2. To reference a page, use the expression `{! $Page.pagename}` to determine its URL.
3. You can then include a link as follows:

```
<apex:outputLink value="{! $Page.AccountDisplay}">I am me!</apex:outputLink>
```

You can think of $Page as a global object that has a field for every page you've created.

Summary

Once you've created your Visualforce page, there are many ways to view it. You can just enter its URL, but you can also make it replace one of the automatically-generated pages, embed it within an existing page layout, or create buttons and hyperlinks that link to it.

Learning More

- Visualforce pages can also be viewed on public-facing web sites by using Force.com Sites. See the Force.com Workbook for an example.
- Sometimes you want to embed links to default actions, such as creating a new Account. Use the `<apex:outputLink>` component together with `URLFOR()` and the `$Action` global variable. For example:

```
<apex:outputLink value="{! URLFOR($Action.Account.new)}">Create</apex:outputLink>
```

Tutorial #7: Customizing User Interface Components

Up until this point you've been modifying Visualforce pages that look and feel like the standard, automatically-generated pages that Force.com produces. Visualforce has a suite of components that produce no styling at all, which you can then style with standard HTML and CSS techniques. In this tutorial you'll learn how to use some of the components that give you full control over the styling of a page.

Step 1: Remove the Header and Sidebar

Create a new Visualforce page and call it `styled`, using the following content:

```
<apex:page standardController="Account">
    <h1>My Styled Page</h1>
    <p>Great!</p>
</apex:page>
```

Now add a few attributes to the `<apex:page>` component. Click **Save** after adding each one to see the effect:

1. Add `sidebar="false"`
2. Add `showHeader="false"`

    The header and sidebar have now been removed, showing a much more basic page. You need to go one step further to remove all default Force.com styling.

3. Add `standardStylesheets="false"`

This ensures that the platform doesn't add any styling at all to the page.

Step 2: Style the HTML with CSS

Using standard web techniques, you can add your own CSS to style the page.

1. Add this just after the `<apex:page>` tag:

```
<style>
    body {font-family: Arial Unicode MS;}
    h1 {color:red;}
</style>
```

Most web designers don't embed CSS, but rather reference an external CSS file. You can do this by using the `<apex:stylesheet>` component.

2. Replace the complete `<style>` section you just added with the following:

```
<apex:stylesheet value="http://developer.force.com/workbooks/vfdemo.css"/>
```

What if you want to host the style files (and accompanying images) themselves on Force.com? You can do that too.

3. Zip your CSS files up, or download this ZIP file as an example.
4. Click **Setup** > **Develop** > **Static Resources** > **New**.
5. Click **New**.
6. In the `Name` field, enter `Style`.
7. In the `File` field, click **Browse** and upload your ZIP file (or the one linked to above).
8. In the `Cache Control` picklist choose **Public**.
9. Now go back to your page and modify your stylesheet component to read as follows:

```
<apex:stylesheet value=" {! URLFOR($Resource.Style, 'styles.css')} "/>
```

The `$Resource` global variable has a field for each static resource that you upload. In this case it references the static resource named style, which is what you assigned to the ZIP file. `URLFOR()` is a formula that constructs URLs—in this example from a static resource and an item within that resource. Now you can modify your stylesheets independently of your web pages by simply replacing the static resources.

Step 3: Iterate Using Unstyled Lists and Tables

You have iterated over a list before in Tutorial #5: Using Standard User Interface Components. The `<apex:pageBlockTable>` component you used produced output that conforms to the standard platform look and feel. Visualforce has a mirror suite of components that allow you to iterate without producing anything other than standard HTML—letting you customize it as you wish.

1. Add the following to your `accountDisplay` Visualforce page:

```
<apex:dataTable value="{!account.contacts}" var="item">
    <apex:column value="{!item.name}"/>
    <apex:column value="{!item.phone}"/>
</apex:dataTable>
```

If you don't see any output, make sure you're passing the identifier of an account as a parameter. The output will look fairly plain when unstyled, but that's the point—you can now style this as you wish with standard CSS.

2. You can also produce a standard HTML unordered list instead of a table by using the `<apex:dataList>` component. Try this:

```
<apex:dataList value="{!account.contacts}" var="item">
    <apex:outputText value="{!item.name}"/>
</apex:dataList>
```

3. If you'd like absolute control, use the `<apex:repeat>` component that simply iterates. You have to do all the outputting yourself. For example, you can mimic the output of the `<apex:dataList>` component as follows:

```
<ul>
    <apex:repeat value="{!account.contacts}" var="item">
```

```
        <li><apex:outputText value="{!item.name}"/></li>
    </apex:repeat>
</ul>
```

Summary

The `showHeader`, `sideBar` and `standardStyleSheets` attributes let you easily modify or simply remove all the standard styling on a Visualforce page, which you can replace with your own CSS, whether embedded or in a referenced static resource. As for components, `<apex:outputText>` lets you output unstylized text, and the `<apex:dataTable>`, `<apex:dataList>`, and `<apex:repeat>` components give you full control over the output when iterating over lists of data.

Learning More

Many components such as `<apex:dataTable>` provide attributes that make it easy to control the style or style class of the component. See for example, the `styleClass` attribute.

Tutorial #8: Inputting Data with Forms

In this tutorial you learn how to create input screens using the standard controller, which provides record save and update functionality out of the box. This introduces you to the major input capabilities and their container—the `<apex:form>` component. Tutorial #13: Creating and Using Custom Controllers extends this and shows how to build forms that interact with your own controllers.

Step 1: Create a Basic Form

The key to any data input is using a form. In this lesson you'll create the most basic form.

1. Create a new Visualforce page called `MyForm`, which uses a standard controller for the Account object.

    ```
    <apex:page standardController="Account">
    </apex:page>
    ```

2. Insert an `<apex:form>` component, into which all your input fields will be placed:

    ```
    <apex:form>
    </apex:form>
    ```

3. Within the form, add an input field for the name field of an account, as well as command button that saves the form when clicked:

    ```
    <apex:inputField value="{! account.name}"/>
    <apex:commandButton action="{! save}" value="Save!"/>
    ```

    This form, although very basic, contains all the essential elements: a form, an input field, and a button that processes the form:

In this case, you use a `<apex:commandButton>` which produces a button. Note that the action element is bound to `{! save}`. This expression language syntax looks similar to the syntax you used to specify a field in a record. However, in this context, it references a method—a piece of code named save. Every standard controller automatically supplies a `save()` method—as well as `update()` and other methods—so in this case, the `save()` method on the standard controller is invoked when the button is clicked.

If you enter a value and click **Save**, the values of the input fields are bound to like-named field values in a new record, and that record is inserted. In other words, the `<apex:inputField>` component produces an input field for the name field of a new account record, and when you click **Save**, ensures that the value you entered is automatically saved to that field.

After you click **Save**, the platform displays the newly-created record. Return to your Visualforce page by entering its URL, which will look something like `https://na6.salesforce.com/apex/MyForm`.

Step 2: Show Field Labels

Visualforce does a lot of work behind the scenes, binding the input field to a field on a new record. It can do more, such as automatically showing the field label (much like `<apex:outputField>` in Tutorial #5: Using Standard User Interface Components), as well as automatically changing the input element to match the data type (for example, showing a picklist instead of an input box).

Modify the contents of the `<apex:form>` element so that it reads as follows:

```
<apex:form>
    <apex:pageBlock>
        <apex:pageBlockSection>
            <apex:inputField value="{!account.name}"/>
            <apex:inputField value="{!account.industry}"/>
            <apex:commandButton action="{!save}" value="Save!"/>
        </apex:pageBlockSection>
    </apex:pageBlock>
</apex:form>
```

By encapsulating the input fields within `<apex:pageBlock>` and `<apex:pageBlockSection>` components, Visualforce automatically inserts field labels ("Account Name", "Industry") as well as indicators of whether values are required for the fields, all using the platform styles.

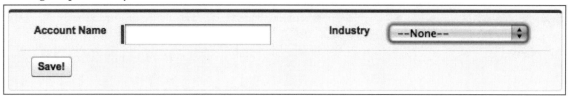

Step 3: Display Warning and Error Messages

The `<apex:pageMessages>` component displays all information, warning or error messages that were generated for all components on the current page. In the previous form, the account name was a required field. To ensure that a standard error message is displayed if someone tries to submit the form without supplying an account name, do the following:

1. Update your page by inserting the following line after the `<apex:pageBlock>` tag:

```
<apex:pageMessages/>
```

2. Now click **Save** on the form. An error panel will be displayed:

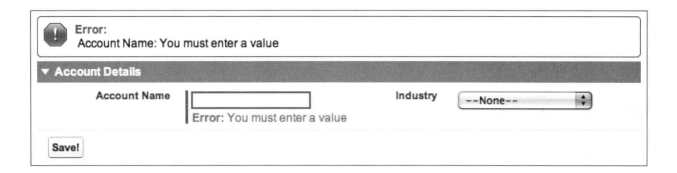

Summary

Visualforce's standard controllers contain methods that make it easy to save and update records. By using the `<apex:form>` and `<apex:inputField>` components, you can easily bind input fields to new records using the standard controllers. The user interface automatically produces input components that match the type of the field—for example displaying a calendar input for a Data type field. The `<apex:pageMessages>` component can be used to group and display the information, warning and error messages across all components in the page.

Learning More

- You can use the `<apex:commandLink>` instead of the `<apex:commandButton>` component within a form to provide a link for form processing.
- Use the `quicksave()` method instead of the `save()` method to insert or update an existing record without redirecting the user to the new record.
- Use the `<apex:pageBlockButtons>` component to place command buttons when using the `<apex:pageBlock>` component.
- Use the `<apex:pageMessage>` component (the singular, not the plural) to create custom messages.

Tutorial #9: Reusing Pages with Templates

Many web sites have a design element that appears on every page, for example a banner or sidebar. You can duplicate this effect in Visualforce by creating a skeleton template that allows other Visualforce pages to implement different content within the same standard structure. Each page that uses the template can substitute different content for the placeholders within the template.

Step 1: Create a Template

Templates are Visualforce pages containing special tags that designate placeholder text insertion positions. In this lesson you create a simple template page that uses the `<apex:insert>` component to specify the position of placeholder text.

1. Create a new Visualforce page called `BasicTemplate`.
2. Use the following as the body of the page:

```
<apex:page>
    <apex:stylesheet value="http://developer.force.com/workbooks/vfdemo.css"/>
    <h1>My Fancy Site</h1>
    <apex:insert name="body"/>
</apex:page>
```

The key here is the `<apex:insert>` component. You won't visit this page (unless developing it) directly. Rather, create another Visualforce page that embeds this template, inserting different values for each of the `<apex:insert>` components. Note that each such component is named. In the above template, you have a single insert position named *body*. You can have dozens of such positions.

Step 2: Use a Template with Another Page

You can now embed the template in a new page, filling in the blanks as you go.

1. Create a new Visualforce page called `MainPage`.
2. Within the page, add the following markup:

```
<apex:page sidebar="false" showHeader="false">
    <apex:composition template="BasicTemplate">
        <apex:define name="body">
            <p>This is a simple page demonstrating that this
               text is substituted, and that a banner is created.</p>
        </apex:define>
    </apex:composition>
</apex:page>
```

The `<apex:composition>` component fetches the Visualforce template page you created earlier, and the `<apex:define>` component fills the named holes in that template. You can create multiple pages that use the same component, and just vary the placeholder text.

Step 3: Include One Visualforce Page within Another

Another way to include content from one page into another is to use the `<apex:include>` component. This lets you duplicate the entire contents of another page, without providing any opportunity to make any changes as you did with the templates.

1. Create a new Visualforce page called `EmbedsAnother`.
2. Use the following markup in the page:

```
<apex:page sidebar="false" showHeader="false">
    <p>Test Before</p>
    <apex:include pageName="MainPage"/>
    <p>Test After</p>
</apex:page>
```

Your original `MainPage` will be inserted verbatim.

Summary

Templates are a nice way to encapsulate page elements that need to be reused across several Visualforce pages. Visualforce pages just need to embed the template and define the content for the placeholders within the template. The `<apex:include>` component provides a simpler way of embedding one page within another.

Learning More

*   Another approach to content reuse is Visualforce Components, covered in Tutorial #10: Creating and Using Custom Components.

Tutorial #10: Creating and Using Custom Components

Up until this point you've been using standard Visualforce components, such as `<apex:dataTable>`. Visualforce has dozens of these components, but sometimes you'll want to create your own. For example, you might want to encapsulate your own custom markup and behavior, which you can reuse on many different Visualforce pages.

Unlike the templates in Tutorial #9: Reusing Pages with Templates, custom components can have their own attributes that can change their appearance on the page in which they're embedded. They can also have complex controller-based logic that executes for that instance of the component. Custom components also automatically become part of the Component Reference help. In short, custom components let you extend Visualforce in whichever direction you see fit.

Step 1: Create a Simple Custom Component

All custom components in Visualforce are wrapped in an `<apex:component>` component. They typically have named attributes, the values of which you can use in the body of your component. In this lesson, you create a component that uses attributes to determine the contents and width of a red box:

1. Click **Setup** > **Develop** > **Components**.
2. Click **New**.
3. In the `Label` and `Name` text boxes, enter `boxedText`.
4. In the Visualforce Markup tab, enter the following:

```
<apex:component>
    <apex:attribute name="text"
            description="The contents of the box."
            type="String" required="true"/>
    <apex:attribute name="borderWidth"
            description="The width of the border."
            type="Integer" required="true"/>

    <div style="border-color:red; border-style:solid; border-width:{! borderWidth}px">
        <apex:outputText value="{! text}"/>
    </div>
</apex:component>
```

5. Click **Quick Save**.

Note how the two attributes are defined to have different types. Visualforce supports a suite of different attribute types and enforces them when someone creates a page that uses the component.

The body of the component can contain other components or simple HTML, as used here—it can also reference the incoming attributes. For example, `{! text}` is substituted with the value of the `text` attribute when using the component.

Step 2: Add a Custom Component to a Visualforce Page

You can now use and reference the component you created in the previous lesson much like any standard Visualforce component. The only difference is that instead of using `apex:` in the name of the component, you use `c:`

1. Create a new Visualforce page called `custom`.
2. Use the following as the body of the page:

```
<apex:page>
    <c:boxedText borderWidth="1" text="Example 1"/>
    <c:boxedText borderWidth="20" text="Example 2"/>
</apex:page>
```

The page simply references the component you created in the previous lesson, twice, each time with different values in the attributes:

Your custom components are automatically added to the help. Click Component Reference and scroll down to `<c:boxedText>`.

Summary

The Visualforce Custom Component functionality lets you build your own components that sit alongside the standard Visualforce components. As components, they can be listed in the Component Reference, have attributes that modify their behavior and appearance, and be reused across multiple Visualforce pages. Custom components can also access controllers (see Tutorial #13: Creating and Using Custom Controllers), letting you take full advantage of Apex.

Tutorial #11: Updating Visualforce Pages with Ajax

Visualforce lets you use Ajax effects, such as partial page updates, without requiring you to implement any complex JavaScript logic. The key element is identifying what needs to be dynamically updated, and then using the `rerender` attribute to dynamically update that region of the page.

Step 1: Identify a Region for Dynamic Updates

A common technique when using Ajax in Visualforce is to group and identify the region to be dynamically updated. The `<apex:outputPanel>` component is often used for this, together with an *id* attribute for identifying the region.

1. Create a Visualforce page called `Dynamic`, using the following body:

```
<apex:page standardController="Account">
    <apex:pageBlock title="{!account.name}">
        <apex:outputPanel id="contactDetails">
            <apex:detail subject="{!$CurrentPage.parameters.cid}"
                relatedList="false" title="false"/>
        </apex:outputPanel>
    </apex:pageBlock>
</apex:page>
```

2. Ensure that your Visualforce page is called with an identifier for a valid account.

Your Visualforce page won't show much at all except for the account name. Note that the `<apex:outputPanel>` has been given an identifier named `contactDetails`. Also note that the `<apex:detail>` component has a `subject` attribute specified. This attribute is expected to be the identifier of the record whose details you want to display. The expression `{! $CurrentPage.parameters.cid}` returns the `cid` parameter passed to the page. Since you're not yet passing in such a parameter, nothing is rendered.

Step 2: Add Dynamic Re-Rendering

Now you need to add elements to the page that set the page parameter and dynamically render the region you've named `detail`:

1. Modify your page by adding a new page block beneath your current one:

```
<apex:pageBlock title="Contacts">
    <apex:form>
        <apex:dataList value="{! account.Contacts}" var="contact">
            {! contact.Name}
        </apex:dataList>
    </apex:form>
</apex:pageBlock>
```

This iterates over the list of contacts associated with the account, creating a list that has the name of each contact.

2. Click **Save**.

If you access your page, you'll see the list of contacts. Now you need to make each contact name clickable.

3. Modify the `{! contact.Name}` expression by wrapping it in an `<apex:commandLink>` component:

```
<apex:commandLink rerender="contactDetails">
    {! contact.Name}
    <apex:param name="cid" value="{! contact.id}"/>
</apex:commandLink>
```

There are two important things about this component. First, it uses a `rerender="contactDetails"` attribute to reference the output panel you created earlier. This tells Visualforce to do a partial page update of that region when the name of the contact is clicked. Second, it uses the `<apex:param>` component to pass a parameter, in this case the `id` of the contact.

If you click any of the contacts, the page dynamically updates that contact, displaying its details, without refreshing the entire page.

Summary

Visualforce provides native support for Ajax partial page updates. The key is to identify a region, and then use the `rerender` attribute to ensure that the region is dynamically updated.

Learning More

There's a lot more to the Ajax and JavaScript support:

- `<apex:actionStatus>` lets you display the status of an Ajax request—displaying different values depending on whether it's in-progress or completed.
- `<apex:actionSupport>` lets you specify the user behavior that triggers an Ajax action for a component. Instead of waiting for an `<apex:commandLink>` component to be clicked, for example, the Ajax action can be triggered by a simple mouse rollover of a label.
- `<apex:actionPoller>` specifies a timer that sends an Ajax update request to Force.com according to a time interval that you specify.
- `<apex:actionFunction>` provides support for invoking controller action methods directly from JavaScript code using an Ajax request.
- `<apex:actionRegion>` demarcates the components processed by Force.com when generating an Ajax request.

Tutorial #12: Using Extensions to Add Functionality

You have already used standard controllers, which provide a set of functionality such as automatic record retrieval, saving, and updating. Sometimes you will want more—perhaps you want to perform additional processing or record retrieval. You can do this by adding a controller extension, which is a custom Apex class that contains functionality that can be accessed from your Visualforce page.

Step 1: Create a Controller Extension

Controller extensions are Apex classes. Creating your first Apex class is as easy as creating your first Visualforce page.

1. Click **Setup** > **Develop** > **Apex Classes**.
2. Click **New**.
3. Enter the following as the body of the Apex class:

```
public class MyExtension {
    private final Account acct;

    public MyExtension(ApexPages.StandardController controller) {
        this.acct = (Account)controller.getRecord();
    }
    public String getTitle() {
        return 'Account: ' + acct.name + ' (' + acct.id + ')';
    }
}
```

This is an Apex class named `MyExtension` that has an instance variable named acct. It has a constructor that retrieves the record from the controller parameter, and saves it in the `acct` variable. The class also has a method called `getTitle()` that returns a string containing the account's name and identifier.

Most extensions have this form—with the constructor being the key ingredient. When the extension is used, Visualforce automatically invokes the constructor, passing in the controller for the page being viewed. This controller provides access to the record being viewed.

Step 2: Add an Extension to a Visualforce Page

Tutorial #8: Inputting Data with Forms shows how to create a very simple form. In this lesson you will duplicate that page, adding the extension functionality:

1. Create a new Visualforce page called `MyAccountWithExtension`.
2. Use the following as the body of the page:

```
<apex:page standardController="Account" extensions="MyExtension">
    <p>{!title}</p>
    <apex:form>
        <apex:inputField value="{!account.name}"/>
        <apex:commandButton action="{!save}" value="Save!"/>
```

```
        </apex:form>
    </apex:page>
```

3. Now access your page with a valid Account identifier passed in as a parameter. Your URL will look something like:

`https://na6.visual.force.com/apex/MyAccountWithExtension?id=0018000000MDfn1`

What you'll find is that your form pre-populates the input field with the name of the identified account. Great! And it also shows your fancy title with the account name and identifier.

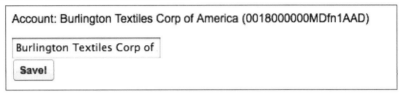

When you save the page, you'll notice that a new line appears above the form. Here's what's happening in your page:

* The attribute `extensions="MyExtension"` ensures that Visualforce instantiates a copy of your Apex class `MyExtension`, passing in a reference to the current controller (you're using the standard controller for Account).
* The syntax `{! title}` instructs Visualforce to look for a method called `getTitle()` and insert the result of calling that method. Because there is such a method in your extension, Visualforce executes it and replaces the statement with the result.

Summary

Controller extensions are Apex classes that extend the functionality of a controller. They allow you to add methods that can be called from your Visualforce pages. A Visualforce page can have more than one extension, and the same extension can be used in multiple Visualforce pages—providing another use case for extensions: as containers for additional functionality for sharing across a number of controllers.

Learning More

* The Apex Language Reference Guide documents the methods available in the `StandardController` class. This lesson uses `getRecord()`. Also available are `cancel()`, `delete()`, `edit()`, `getId()`, `save()`, and `view()`.
* For an introduction to the Apex programming language, read the Apex Workbook.

Tutorial #13: Creating and Using Custom Controllers

Tutorial #4: Using Standard Controllers introduced how Visualforce supports the Model-View-Controller (MVC) style of user interface creation. Controllers typically retrieve the data to be displayed in a Visualforce page, and contain code that executes in response to page actions, such as a command button being clicked. Up until this point, you've been using a standard controller—a set of logic provided for you out of the box by the platform. In this tutorial you create your own controller by writing Apex code.

Step 1: Create a Page with a Controller

You create controllers the same way you created extensions in the previous tutorial, by navigating to **Setup** > **Develop** > **Apex Classes** > **New**. You can also have the Visualforce editor create them for you.

1. Create a new Visualforce page named `AccountWithContacts`.
2. Enter the following as the body of the page:

```
<apex:page controller="MyController">
    <apex:form>
        <apex:dataList value="{! myaccounts}" var="acct">
            <apex:outputText value="{! acct.name}"/>
        </apex:dataList>
    </apex:form>
</apex:page>
```

The contents of the page will be very familiar to you. The primary component iterates over a list of accounts, displaying their names. Where is `myaccounts` defined? It's not defined yet, but it will reside in the controller that you specified, `MyController`.

3. Click **Save**.
4. Visualforce notes that the class `MyController` doesn't exist. Click **Create Apex class 'public class MyController'**.
5. Visualforce notes that there's an unknown property `myaccounts` and offers to create it for you. Click **Create Apex method 'MyController.getMyAccounts'**.

You will notice two things in your Visualforce editor. First, there's another error message: `Unknown property 'String.name'`. This happens because you haven't quite fully defined the `getMyAccounts()` method yet. Visualforce doesn't know the type that will be returned by that method. You'll also notice a new tab has appeared next to Page Editor titled Controller. This lets you modify the controller's Apex class.

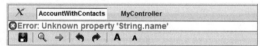

Step 2: Add a Method to Retrieve Account Records

You're now ready to write `getMyAccounts()`, which simply returns the list of 10 accounts most recently modified.

1. Click the **MyController** tab.

2. Modify the `getMyAccounts()` method to read as follows:

```
public List<Account> getMyAccounts() {
    return [SELECT Id, Name, AccountNumber FROM Account ORDER BY
            LastModifiedDate DESC LIMIT 10];
}
```

3. Click **Save**.

Your page now displays the names of the 10 most recently modified accounts. The Visualforce expression `{! myaccounts}` causes Visualforce to execute your `getMyAccounts()` method in the MyController class. That method returns a list of account records, which is what the `<apex:dataList>` component iterates over.

Step 3: Add an Action Method to a Controller

In this lesson you add an action method, a method that is invoked when the user of your Visualforce page clicks on a button or link. You previously used such a method, `save()`, on the standard controller—now you'll write your own. The goal is to modify the page to dynamically display a selected account record's list of contacts.

1. Click **MyController** to edit the controller for your Visualforce page.
2. Below the line `public class MyController {` add the following two lines:

```
public Id selectedAccount { get; set; }
public List<Contact> contactsInformation { get; set; }
```

This creates two properties. The first, `selectedAccount`, is an identifier, while the second, `contactsInformation`, is a list of Contact records.

3. Click **AccountWithContacts** to edit the Visualforce page, and add the following snippet just below the `</apex:form>` line:

```
<apex:outputPanel id="ContactDetail">
    <apex:repeat value="{! contactsInformation}" var="contact">
        <p>{! contact.FirstName & ' ' & contact.LastName}</p>
    </apex:repeat>
</apex:outputPanel>
```

This iterates over the list of contacts (remember, `contactsInformation` is defined to return `List<Contact>`), displaying their first and last names.

At this point, you can save the page and you'll notice no change. What you need to do now is ensure that when an account name is clicked, the `contactsInformation` property is populated with that account record's contacts.

4. Modify your controller by clicking **MyController** and adding the following before the final brace:

```
public void accountClicked() {
    contactsInformation = [SELECT FirstName, LastName FROM Contact
            WHERE AccountID = :selectedAccount];
}
```

5. Replace the line `<apex:outputText value="{! acct.name}"/>` in your Visualforce page with the following:

```
<apex:commandlink action="{! accountClicked}" rerender="ContactDetail">
    <apex:outputText value="{! acct.name}"/>
    <apex:param name="id" value="{! acct.Id}" assignTo="{!selectedAccount}"/>
</apex:commandLink>
```

This uses the `rerender` attribute to ensure that the output panel is refreshed using an Ajax update.

6. Click **Save**.

Now when you select an account record with related contacts, the contacts for that record are dynamically displayed below the list of accounts.

A lot happens when you click the name of an account:

- Because an `<apex:param>` component is supplied, the ID of the current account is first assigned to the property `selectedAccount` in the controller. So now the controller knows which account you selected.

- Because the account name is wrapped in an `<apex:commandLink>` component, the method indicated in the action attribute, `accountClicked()`, is invoked.

- When the `accountClicked()` method runs, it performs a simple query, using the `selectedAccount` identifier, and assigns the result to the `contactsInformation` property.

- Because the `<apex:commandLink>` component has a `rerender` attribute, the output panel dynamically renders, which in turn iterates over the `contactsInformation` and displays the contacts' names.

That's a lot to digest! Take your time, experimenting by removing attributes, modifying the methods, and noting what changes occur. Also, refer back to Tutorial #11: Updating Visualforce Pages with Ajax to learn more about the Ajax effect.

Summary

Custom controllers contain custom logic and data manipulation that can be used by a Visualforce page. For example, a custom controller can retrieve a list of items to be displayed, make a callout to an external web service, validate and insert data, and more—and all of these operations will be available to the Visualforce page that uses it as a controller.

Learning More

- Read the Apex Workbook to learn the basics of programming in Apex.
- Check out the Apex Language Reference Guide for a complete guide.

Addendum

Congratulations on completing the workbook! You are now familiar with the major bits and pieces that make up Visualforce. Visualforce can do much more: for example you can use it to render a page as a PDF, access and manipulate page query parameters, build advanced dashboard components, define email templates, handle pagination, and build the pages in a Force.com Site. With the basics in this workbook mastered, you're ready to tackle it all!

Notes